All the World's a Pub!

Jim Green and Bill Tidy

*The **only** poetry book that offers the chance of*

FREE BEER!

All the World's a Pub!

(why do poetry books have the title repeated just inside? Do the publishers think the reader has forgotten it already? Then again - perhaps you have!)

First published in 2003 by James Green Publishing 2 Newburn Holdings nr. Berwick Upon Tweed and printed in Great Britain by JW Arrowsmith Ltd, Bristol.
Reprinted 2003

© cartoons Bill Tidy 2003
© Jim and Frank Green and contributors 2003

ISBN 0 9515056 8 8

This book is dedicated to good beer, good pubs and all those who can tell the difference especially:

Frank Green 1949-2000

By the same authors

Nothing else, as yet, thank goodness!

At last! A poetry anthology that brings you the great poems from the great writers:

Alfred Lord Tennisracket, A. E. Housemartin, Slattey Lengrow, Jack Buckett, Robert Louis Hornblower, Wilfred Shakespeare, 'Big' Nelly Applegate, Lenny Spavin the Irish Wonder Poet, Tom......
and many more too far gone to mention.

Oh yes, and a few other has-beens who wanted to be allowed in:

Robert Browning, William Blake, Dr. Samuel Johnson, Edgar Allan Poe and a bloke called John Milton or it may have been Milton John, one or the other anyway.

But you can miss them out if you want to.

The reviews speak for themselves

'This book....' Chesney Wallop,
The Review of Modern Literature.

'One does not often come upon such a book.'
Eremont Pile, *The Aesthete.*

'This book could be for poetry what the San
Andreas fault is for San Francisco.'
Lydia Spoons, *Verse Weekly.*

'This is the greatest book since 'Pubs that give
Credit'. We must have more of this.'
Sosthenes, *The Sheffield and South Yorkshire
Snuff Breeders' Gazette.*

'First editions of this book, indeed any
editions of this book, are likely to be very rare
in the future.'
Lucifer, *The Matchbox and Lighter Collectors'
Yearbook.*

All the World's a Pub!

The world's first authoritative anthology of authentic Beer Poetry

(try saying that at 10.30pm!)

CONTENTS

Introduction 1

The Poetry Begins 3

An Outbreak of Dramatic Verse 13

The Origins of Beer Poetry 21

Meanwhile, back at the ranch... 27

Great Literature 31

Back at the ranch..., again 41

The Japanese Equivalent of the Limerick 45

The End 47

An Insider View 53

Modern Verse!!!!!! 61

Bad Poetry 67

The Beginning of The End 73

Part 2 of The End (the *FREE BEER* bit) 77

The End of The End 81

Introduction

I think it was the poet Pope who said, "The proper study of man is man." Or it may have been 'Fast' Willie Snubbs - anyway it was certainly 'Fast' Willie who wrote those immortal lines;

What? No beer?
I'm out of here!

which, if not great poetry, certainly makes its point. You can see what they both meant, of course.

Serious writing of any sort has to be about the things that really matter. Poetry, as a serious writing form, has a tendency to come and go in the fashion stakes. You get great wodges of time when everybody seems to be rhyming like mad, others when vers libre or poetry that doesn't rhyme is all around you. Then the bottom drops out of the market completely and you get poets, coughing blood and standing outside publishers' offices, trying to sell you, 'The Big Verse'. Well, as Paul Verlaine said, "Et tout le reste est Littérature!" or "Literature! What a way to earn a bloody living!" (of course it loses something in the translation). And he should know, he was a French poet and tougher than that it does not come, believe me.

But one quiet area of poetry goes on and on - Beer Poetry. It avoids fashion. It is a literary style that allies itself to a way of life. It talks of the happy pint, the convivial hotel bar, the good pub, the dreamy drink, the way things might be, not the way things are (sorry, I unintentionally and prematurely burst into verse there). Beer Poetry is the highest form of literature known to - well, anyone who likes beer. But Beer Poetry is not only great literature, it is also true! Everyone who likes a pint finds themselves and their deepest joys and fears in Beer Poetry and not only themselves but everyone else and all life's situations. If you don't believe me then read on - and as Titus 'Two Bladders' Andronicus famously said in the Flag and Bottle pub, "Another pint, please, Gavin. It's been a difficult day."

The return home of Titus 'Two Bladders' Andronicus.

Look, sunshine, when is the bloody poetry going to start? Only, you see I thought this was a poetry book and here I am on page 3 and there's still no poetry. How much more flannel do I have to wade through before I get sight of something that rhymes or even a bit of blank verse because if I don't get something soon....

Alright, alright, keep your shirt on. I've had to wash my pen through and let the ink settle. I use pen-conditioned ink mate, not your modern rubbish in little plastic tubes and in weather like this the paper can get damp and...

Poetry NOW or I'll...

Alright, alright, what a lot of fuss about a bit of poetry.

My Lords, ladies and gentlemen. In the blue corner with the drawing pad – Mr. Bill 'I bought the last round didn't I?' Tidy. And in the Red Corner with the chewed biro Jimmy 'Chalk this one up will you, Gavin?' Green.

Right gents, no biting or gouging and keep the poetry as clean as you can.

Ladies and gentlemen –

THE POETRY BEGINS!

Why beer?

Why beer? you ask.
Why favour the liquid from the cask?
Why ale? You say.
Why does that drink make your day?
Why not wine?
Why not the red divine?
Why not a rare white?
Why not a pale delight?

Well, you ask me 'Why?'
So I reply. Beer it must be.
Beer for me.
Beer in all its varied glory.
Beer for a rambling, pub-told story.
Beer laughs, beer's jolly.
Beer's for gentle folly.

Beer's friendly and takes no airs.
Beer doesn't count the years.
No '98 or '82.
No silly cost, no premier cru,
Beer is honest, beer is fun.
Beer is beer for everyone.
All drinkers equal under the sun.

So, don't ask 'why?'
Just get some in.
Bring on the pints
And let's begin.

Alfred Lord Tennisracket

WHY BEER?

'Why Beer,' you ask.

Robinson Crusoe

He sits upon the coral strand,
so full of ale he cannot stand.
He's emptied the wreck
of its dark oak kegs,
carried them ashore on nerveless legs,
But he waves not at ships however near,
This old sailor won't share his beer.

Robert Louis Hornblower

Once

Once, when I was young and hot
I wanted fame and money,
I wanted the lot.
I wanted drinks
that came in funny glasses,
I wanted to score
when I made passes.
Now, when I am not so young,
and cool,
I'll settle for good beer, good pubs,
good friends
and be myself,
happy who was once
a fool.

Charlie O' Shaugnessey

Dad, tell me about beer.

Is all ale pale?
No, it can be dark.
And strong?
Oh yes, very strong.

Is all beer bitter?
No, it can be sweet.
Is that a fault?
No, it's the malt.

Is lager really beer?
Does it give cheer?
Of course.
Then never fear, it's beer.

What do hops do?
They give bitterness
to the brew
and make it keep.

Anything else?
Induce sleep.
I thought that was the alcohol?
No, not at all.

Hops, as a soporific,
are gentle but terrific.
So is beer the best?
Oh yes, the best, better than all the rest.

So take the pint
I've bought you, son,
It isn't every day
you're twenty one.

Stanley Grudge

When I die

When I die, please can I go
to a place I've seen quite often,
to a place I feel I know?
It's a place of peace and perfection,
a place of laughter and light,
where the days are always sunny,
and the future's always bright.
I don't want to go to heaven
and play a harp or sing.
I don't want to sit with a crowd on a cloud
or any of that sort of thing.
Can I go where I'll be happy,
where goodness will abound ?
A summer Sunday lunchtime pub,
when it's somebody else's round.

Lenny Spavin

Reflections

You do not see yourself reflected
in a pint of good beer.
The thin foam won't let you.
You can be anyone, for a time,
with a good pint of beer,
anyone your happy mind will let you.
And as the pint goes down in the glass
as the quiet, thoughtful, moments pass
you can think of any future.
And when the raised glass
tilts to a finish, reflect -
Now you see only darkly,
through the bottom of a glass.
Now the pint is ended.

Dudley Walkinshaw

Destiny

Beer for me!
Just one pint and I could plainly see.
My future was unfurled -
I went and conquered
All the Eastern World!

attributed to Alexander the Great, King of Macedonia, High King of Persia, Lord of the Peacock Throne, born at 52 Acacia Avenue, Wolverhampton, Staffordshire. Died of unknown causes, among many empty pint glasses at The Beard and Curlers, Babylon 422 B.C., with his bar bill unpaid!

Thank God.

Thank God for good beer
and sunshine on a green landscape.
For golden summer days,
for meadows and country pathways.

Thank God for pubs at walking's end
where you can sit and take your ease,
and drink the golden beer
and feel the joy of rest and cheer.

Thank God for good beer
and England in the sun.

A. E. Housemartin

AN OUTBREAK OF
DRAMATIC VERSE

Poetry, even Beer Poetry, comes in all shapes and sizes. We have seen in the first poems in this book examples of the poem simple and straightforward - a celebration of the lovely liquid.

But Beer is not all about skittles, it is about life! And Beer Poetry has never flinched from holding up a true mirror to the human condition. This is, perhaps, seen in its most alarming form when poetry is married to the drama and you get dramatic verse.

Dramatic verse or, for the layman, plays that rhyme, were popular once (no-one seems to know why!) but have, thankfully, died out. The last known outbreak was recorded in London in the 1930s.

What follows is an early piece of dramatic verse from the 17th century. It deals, as all great drama should, with those issues central to life itself. Give it a miss if you are frail or of a nervous disposition. Certainly do not try to read it without a pint in front of you.

You have been warned!

"In sooth, we was robbed."

*(Saturday evening in November. The Flag and Bottle,
Stratford. Enter a varlet wearing a Stratford on Avon
United scarf)*

Eftsoons, ecod, but give me beer,
the team's gone down
and I need cheer.
The ref. was blind
the linesmen bent.
I wish they were to hell
quick sent.

(the landlord places a pint before the varlet, who drinks)

For first half forty minutes
we were best.
Their defence so weak
we took it for a jest.
Yet could we score?
But for the vilest luck
We'd have had four.

(The varlet pauses and drinks deeply)

Then, one short minute
before the half-time whistle blew
their goal-hanging centre-forward
wriggled through.
The long ball from the middle sent
and we, as one, rose and the air was rent
when all good men stood up and cried,
Offside! Offside!
'Not so,' the white-sticked whistler said
and pointed to the centre spot instead.

(the varlet breaks down and, ordering another pint, continues with difficulty)

And so it stayed
for all the game.
How hard we played,
how well we stayed.
I tell thee what,
it's a crying shame how little we got,
it's all part of a ***** plot.

(the varlet revives, takes a drink and turns to address the assembled throng of thinkers and drinkers)

And so I say, give me more beer
and let me hear all the good cheer.
Of other teams, better served,
of wins deserved.
Of how Lancaster overcame York
or the other way about.

Well, what of the play?
Let us all drink and say,
Tomorrow is another day! (cheering)

(the varlet is bought another pint by the happy mob and tells them of what great feats Stratford on Avon United will perform on the field of battle the following week, away to Spittalfield Rovers managed by Frankie 'The Pen' Bacon.)

attributed to Wilfred Shakespeare (cousin to somebody whose name I forget)

Here's another from a slightly later date.

The Needy Knifegrinder.

Cast:
Friend of Humanity, a well-off, well-educated liberal.
Knife grinder, definitely of the people.

Friend of Humanity:

Needy Knife-grinder! Whither are you going?
Rough is the road, your wheel is out of order -
Bleak blows the blast;
your hat has got a hole in it,
So have your breeches!

Weary knife-grinder! Little think the proud ones,
who in their coaches roll along the turnpike-road,
what hard work 'tis all day crying,
Knives and Scissors to grind O.

Tell me, Knife-grinder,
how came you to grind knives?
Did some rich man tyranically use you?
Was it the squire, or the parson of the parish?
Or the attorney?

Was it the squire for killing his game?
Or the covetous parson
for his tithes distraining?
Or roguish lawyer
made you lose your little
all in a lawsuit?

Have you not read
'The Rights of Man' by Thomas Paine?
Drops of compassion tremble on my eyelids'
ready to fall as soon
as you have told me your pitiful story.

Knife Grinder:

Story! God bless you,
I have none to tell, sir.
Only last night a-drinking
at the Flag and Bottle
this poor old hat and breeches,
as you see,
were torn in a scuffle.
Constables came up
for to take me into custody;
they took me before the justice.

Justice Pepperpot put me
in the parish stocks for a vagrant.
I should be glad to drink
your honour's health in a pot of beer,
if you will give me sixpence;
but for my part, I never meddle
with Politics, sir!

Friend of Humanity:

I, give thee sixpence!
I will see thee damn'd first -
Wretch! Whom no sense of wrongs
can rouse to vengeance;
Sordid, unfeeling, reprobate;
degraded, spiritless outcast!

*(Kicks the Knife-grinder, overturns his wheel, and
exits in a transport of Republican enthusiasm and
universal philanthropy)*

*George Canning 1770 - 1827 and J. H. Frere
1769 - 1846 (in imitation of the poet Robert*

Southey and as a spoof on supporters in England of the Republicanism of the French Revolution)

It should be mentioned here that the poet George Canning is the same George Canning who was Foreign Secretary in 1807 and 1822 when Napoleon was making such a nuisance of himself across Europe and upsetting all right-minded people.

I somehow get the feeling that politicians must have been a little different in those days from what rolls off the production line today. 'Wee' Georgie Canning could not only sort out Napoleon (with the help of Arthur Wellesley - look him up!) but sort out Europe after all the noise had died down and still find time to write stuff that is quite good.

What have we got today? A good question. I wish we had a good answer.

In passing, did you know...

In the first translation of the Bible into English, by John Wycliffe in the 14th century, it is written,

'for he schal be gret before the Lord; and he schal not drinke wyn ne sydyr.'

Well, you can't say fairer than that, those elements of fallen humanity who wilfully forsake honest beer for wine (wyn) or cider (sydyr) shall definitely *not* be great before the Lord – not me saying it, mind you, but John Wycliffe – makes you think, doesn't it?

THE ORIGINS OF BEER
POETRY

In much the same way that no-one is sure just when or where beer first appeared no-one can quite place the blame for the first outbreak of poetry. However, we can be certain that beer came before poetry because no right minded person would commit poetry to paper (or stone) without having had a couple of pints first.

No really early beer poetry survives. Beer, mead or ale gets a mention by people like Chaucer or the bloke who wrote Beowulf but they wrote in gibberish so that doesn't count. Early beer poetry was probably erased by envious wine bibbers during the Roman occupation. Our earliest domestic poetry comes to us in the form of medieval songs:

Sumer is icumen in -Lhude sing, cuccu!

This is 13th century drivel and, from the spelling, certainly written after several pints of strong ale! However, not all early song poetry was written after drinking. By the 16th century they had learnt to write before they started drinking so at least their spelling had improved.

Bring us in good ale

Bring us in no brown bread,
for that is made of bran,
Nor bring us in no white bread,
for therein is no gain,
But bring us in Good Ale!

Bring us in no beef,
for there are many bones,
but bring us in Good Ale,
for that goes down at once,
And bring us in Good Ale!

Bring us in no bacon,
for that is passing fat,
But bring us in Good Ale,
and give us enough of that,
And bring us in Good Ale!

Bring us in no eggs,
for there are many shells,
But bring us in Good Ale,
and give us nothing else,
And bring us in Good Ale!

*There are about 47 more verses covering every food
known to man but I think you get the idea, they want
Good Ale!*

Anon 16th century

Ale

Here's to jolly good ale and old,
which makes the feeble healthy
and maketh the craven bold.

Bishop of Bath and Wells 19th cent.

We had bishops who talked sense then!

Beer and Faith

Heresy and beer
came hopping into England
in a year.

(on the arrival of Lutheranism and Dutch hops in 1492)

*I should point out here, that this poem was sent in by 'Big'
Nelly Applegate from her unpublished book;*
       *'European Social History as revealed through its
doggerel'.*
       *It is included only for its poetic merit not its historical
accuracy and the management cannot accept any
responsibility for any bets lost in pubs as a result of using
the dates given. I thank you.*

MEANWHILE,
BACK AT THE RANCH…

Truly beautiful

Some beer is truly beautiful,
it has a taste, such a taste,
and such a colour.

Some beer is wonderful.
I know it has
the same sad side effects
as its poor relations,
wines and spirits.
But its company is so different.

Some beer is truly beautiful.

Jack Buckett

A two pint story

He was telling a two pint story,
the sort that rambles
and gets lost,
and then will re-appear.
A story that goes well with beer.

It was a summer Sunday story
told to friends over cool pints
in the easy pub shade
before the midday meal,
a story you don't so much listen to as feel.

It featured an epic struggle with a lawnmower,
a clash of Titans on the front lawn.
It was told in a drowsy summer haze
when friends sit quietly
and listen in a happy daze.

The way he told it everyone could see
that great things had been done on that lawn,
that right had triumphed in the face of might.
No blood spilt, true, but honour upheld
- quite!

And, at the end, they went their separate ways.
To summer Sunday lunch
and perhaps a glass of wine.
But they had enjoyed the two pint story.
And what is better, they felt, than friends, pints
and summer glory?

Chervill Boltardy

Hack writer in a pub at evening.

Gentlemen, ladies,
may you all go to Hades!

I do not like what you pay me to do
I do not like being untrue
to the artist – myself – I thank you.
Sir (me), my health.

I do not like being a literary whore
and, what's more,
I won't, not any more.
I'll write what I want
and if you don't like it, I don't care,
so there!

I won't, can't, shouldn't -
admittedly did – for money,
but now the tin lid.
I won't any more.

I'll write...I'll write....something.
Something great and good,
I'll write what I should.
I'll write - well I will, you'll see,
I may even write poetry.
You wait, you'll surely hear from me.

Anyone got the time?
Really! Time for one more then.
Another pint please, Gavin.
Thanks.

'Little' Jimmy Green

GREAT LITERATURE
(plus interlude)

What, exactly, is great literature? And - following on from that - what makes a great writer? Everyone clever knows, of course, but they won't tell you. It's your own fault you don't know, you're a philistine and a twit - too dull or common to see what is obvious to everyone of culture. Oh, well!

Beer Poetry has suffered less than many forms of writing from 'art' and consequently its great names; Alfred Lord Tennisracket, 'Big' Nelly Applegate, Stanley Grudge and Charlie 'The Snout' O'Shaugnessey, do not get a mention in the Dictionary of National Biography (don't pretend you've heard of it let alone read it!). But the great and the good sometimes wrote Beer Poetry and here is some of it.

If you like it, well - each to his own. But, really, compared to the other stuff in this book, do you think it's GREAT LITERATURE?

To Nelson, in beer!

Here's to Nelson's memory!
'Tis the second time that I, at sea,
Right off Cape Trafalgar here,
Have drunk it deep in British Beer.
Nelson for ever - any time
I am his to command in prose or rhyme!
Give me of Nelson only a touch,
And I save it, be it little or much:
Here's one our captain gives, and so
Down at the word it shall go!

Robert Browning

<u>The Little Vagabond</u>
An extract

...if at church they would give us some ale,
And a pleasant fire our souls to regale,
We'd sing and we'd pray all the live-long day,
Nor ever once wish from the church to stray.
Then the parson might preach, and drink, and sing,
And we'd be as happy as birds in the spring.

William Blake

(Archbishop of Canterbury please note — nothing has changed!!!)

Here's something from an American who is better known for his more sombre work. This poem is evidence, if more were needed, that the writer's muse is not some skimpily clad Greek floozy who flits about and only turns up when she feels like it rather than when she is wanted. The true muse is a pint of the right stuff at the right time!

Fill with mingled cream and amber,
I will drain that glass again.
Such hilarious visions clamber
Through the chambers of my brain.
Quaintest thoughts, queerest fancies
Come to life and fade away;
What care I how time advances?
I am drinking ale today.

Edgar Allan Poe

At this point we take a brief break from GREAT ART.

The Haven

What if the wild winds threaten?
What if the rain pours down?
I laugh to scorn the branches torn
and the tiles thrown round the town.
For I have peace a plenty
inside while the night is wild.
I'm safe and snug in my local pub
with a pint of delicious Mild.

'Big' Nelly Applegate

Now back to the ART....

Imitation in the style of ****

Hermit hoar, in solemn cell
Wearing out life's evening grey;
Strike thy bosom, Sage, and tell
What is bliss, and which the way?

Thus I spoke, and speaking, sigh'd
Scarce repressed the starting tear,
when the hoary sage replied,
Come in my lad, and drink some beer!

Samuel Johnson

(It's in imitation of somebody, but I don't know who and even if I did, I doubt if I could see the joke!)

The poet John Milton is famous for having lost Paradise but, luckily, he found it again. I think he had left it in his other trousers, I'm sure it was something like that. We've all woken up and found that we can't find something although we are sure we had it last night at the pub. Anyway he is big in the poetry line but, strangely if he had found Paradise, he didn't write much about beer. Here is his only known bit:

When the merry bells ring round,
And the jocund rebecks sound
To many a youth and many a maid
Dancing in the chequered shade;
And young and old come forth to play
On a sunshine holiday
Till the livelong daylight fail:
Then to spicy nut-brown ale.

John Milton (or Milton John)

A 'rebeck' by the way is an old form of bottle-opener which caused the beer bottle to give a loud 'pop' when it was opened causing much innocent amusement and jollity.

The above information is taken from 'A Concise History of Beer Bottles and Associated items' by Arnold Ale-Burger to be published as soon as he can find a vanity publisher who works on credit or note-of-hand.

But not all the 'greats' were so modern. The following poem was written about the battle of Cattraeth between the invading Saxons and the native Britons. I leave you to work out why the Brits lost.

The warriors marched to Cattraeth,
full of words.
Bright mead gave them pleasure,
their bliss was their bane.

The warriors marched to Cattraeth,
full of mead.
Drunken, but firm in array,
Great was the shame.

For the sweetness of the mead,
In the day of our need,
Is now our bitterness,
Blunts all our arms for the strife,
Is a friend of the lip
But a foe to the life.

I drank Mordei's mead,
I drank, and now for that,
I bleed.

Aneurin

MEANWHILE....

BACK AT THE RANCH THE
POETRY CONTINUES
UNABATED!

Bravery and Beer

Courage given by beer
removes a man's fear
and can only fail
if he runs out of ale!

Arnold Ale-Burger

Pub Talk

If shy, ale will make you audacious,
and witty and wise,
and somewhat
Lokwayshush (hic!)

Arnold Ale-burger

Helpline

The lawn needs cutting,
the edges 'strimmed',
the house bricks 'pointed',
hedges trimmed.
"I'll do it all, love,
and never fail,
but first just one pull
of hand drawn Ale!"

Germain St. Verdant

This kind of poetry is called 'Social Realism' and is in a style which dates from the 1950s or 60s when a bloke, whose name I forget, wrote a play, the title of which I can't recall, about a middle-class young bloke called something or other who got upset a lot and shouted at his two best friends. It made a big splash at the time although I could never see what there was in it, I mean it wasn't like any real life as me and my mates lived it. We went down the Locarno ballroom mostly and didn't shout at each other too much about anything.

Still, there you are, 'Social Realism', or 'Kitchen Sink' as it was sometimes known, has had its look in and now we can get on.

Are you annoyed at the pace of change? Do you sigh for lost quality? Can you lend me five quid 'til next Friday? Let us reassure you that good standards can still be found in a world of shifting values.

Tradition

A good thing never lasts, they say
and perhaps what they say is true.
But some things last
handed on from the past
handed on for me and you.
I'll name you one that goes on and on
and has never been known to fail
An honest pint that tastes just right,
a pint of fine Old Ale.

Lady Lavinia Dishpot

THE JAPANESE
EQUIVALENT OF THE
LIMERICK

Do you know what a Haiku is? Well I'll tell you anyway. A Haiku is a form of Japanese verse, which need not necessarily rhyme, but must contain exactly seventeen syllables. (this definition is provided by Arnold Ale-Burger and should not be relied upon!) Not quite as simple as the Limerick, is it?

Quite why some people, even whole countries, feel the need to make the difficult job of writing poetry even more difficult I cannot say - but - here is a Haiku:

I've drunk 'Tcha'ya, and Saki too,
but when in Britain, a strong, brown brew.

Tu Fiu Grogi

That's it for the Orient, by the way, we can't see this book selling thousands farther east than King's Lynn so one is enough as far as we're concerned.

THE END

(not the real end, of course, that comes at the end. This is another The End)

please read this section bare-headed.

Many people feel the urge to write poetry with the result that poetry can be found in many different places. Books, like this one, may be its respectable home but books are not really the natural home of poetry. This is because poets fall into two categories; those who write for themselves and those who write for a public.

Private poets are like secret drinkers and should be pitied rather than blamed. If private poets offer to read any poems to you, respect their privacy and refuse to listen. Public poets, however, cannot be suppressed, they always find a way. The earliest form of art was graffiti and poets are still at it! There must be an artistic difference between the rhymed obscenity in a public toilet written by a disturbed mind and the daring verse of the dissident on a police state public wall. Are they very distant cousins?

Epitaphs, however, are a more acceptable form of public poetry, they are, after all, the last word!

Epitaph for a Brewer

Here lies poor Burton,
He was both 'ale and stout;
Death laid him on this bitter bier.
Now in 'eaven 'e hops about.

*This cunning play on words may be too subtle for most
readers so if you can't see the puns that are in it take it
along to someone clever like any Aussie student doing bar
work and have it explained to you.*

*That way you can tell it to your mates and explain it to
them when they don't understand and put on dog about your
superior command of English. You never know they might be
so impressed they'll forget it's your round.*

meanwhile...

"There'll always be an England, as long as there's English beer," so my old dad told me. So, if it's your round, mine's a pint.

Celebration

England, Oh England,
fields and lanes and towns,
wild and weathered uplands,
gently rolling downs.
How shall I rejoice, then,
at the glory that is here?
I'll sit back and think of England
with a pint of English beer.

When sitting for this work of art I insisted that Mr. Tidy not show my face so that I could still walk about in public after I became a famous poet. That's the sort of humble person I am.

Epitaphs in Coventry University Grounds
(formerly a church graveyard)

Tom who lies here
is resting from -BEER
(probably by his wife)

Stranger; read and pause to think.
Eat not too much, and seldom DRINK.
God doth not always warnings give,
And so be careful how YOU live.
(probably by his wife, and maybe Tom's as well)

AN INSIDER VIEW

*(containing previously unpublished correspondence
of vital importance to understanding the
development of
Tudor literature and the centrality of
beer in the success of Shakespearian drama.)*

Literature is a funny business. Some people make a sack-full of money, whilst others, equally talented, get nowhere. I can't tell you how it works, nor I suspect can anyone else. One poet dies penniless in the gutter and another poet, pulling down a six-figure royalty but with no more talent, steps over the body on his way to his agent. They say that while other writers often borrow ideas, poets steal. That's literature, folks!

And in Beer Poetry we are sometimes privileged to see behind the scenes and see how the stuff we have now actually got written. You won't get any of this in the respectable anthologies but the word is passed down from father to son in pubs across the road; "I once knew somebody who had it from a friend whose wife took in the washing for a man who...",

Well, suffice to say it is as reliable as everything anybody ever heard in a pub.

All the world's a pub

All the world's a pub
and all the people drinkers.
They have their exits and their entrances
and one man in his time
drinks many pints.

First the youth
boastful and unsure
who orders odd drinks
that taste like manure.
Then the young man
bearded like the pard
who drinks often and hard.

Then the man of middle age
who in drink has become more sage
who learns by care
the nature of each brew
and settles to drink just a few.

Finally the oldie
sitting in his place
who gently drinks his pint
with joy and grace
and watches youngsters
muscle to the bar
and grins and remembers times afar

And mutters what we
all eventually know
'Twas ever thus,
'twas always, e'en so.

Wilfred Shakespeare

copy to Francis Bacon.

C/o The Flag and Bottle
Dung Street
Stratford on Avon
Warks.

Dear Mr. Bacon,

Is there any market for my style of writing? (I enclose a poem written to my cousin William) I feel I might make a living knocking out this stuff. What do you think?

Yr. Ob. Serv. W. Shakespeare

P.S. I enclose a s.a.e.

From Francis Bacon Esq.
C/o The Cutpurse and Mackerel
off Threadneedle Street
London

Dear Wilfred,

     I regret there is no market for this kind of
verse. I suggest you do not give up your job as a
vermin instructor. However, please send me copies of
any other poems you write as my old penniless mother
seems to enjoy them.
I remain yrs. etc., etc.

     Frankie Bacon

From William Shikspoke,
C/o The Frog and Nightgown
off Canary Wharf
London

Will, more of the same please. With the new spelling of my name I think I can make a go of it as a writer.

By the way, what's pard?

P.S. Don't let Frankie 'The Pen' Bacon see any of this.
He is not to be trusted!

To drink or not to drink

To drink or not to drink,
that is the question.
Whether 'tis nobler in the mind
to drink,
or eat and risk indigestion.
To drink, to sleep,
aye there's the rub.
In drink we end the heart ache
and the thousand natural shocks
that flesh is heir to.
To sleep,
to sleep perchance to dream,
and in that beery sleep
what dreams may come
must give us pause,
and so
although my thirst bid me drink
my conscience doth command me, no!
Thus conscience doth
make cowards of us all.
And the native hue of resolution
is sicklied o'er with
the pale cast of thought.
So, sod the thinking, Bill,
let's go and get on with the drinking!

*Wilfred Shakespeare (to his cousin William inviting
him and his friends to the Flag and Bottle tavern,
Stratford on Avon and believed to have had an influence
on one of William's plays)*

MODERN VERSE !!!!!!

Abandon hope all ye who enter here.

No book of poetry, not even a book of Beer Poetry,
can ignore –

Modern Verse!

Modern verse began around 1910 when a lot of nasty
things happened in 'art'. You got groups like the
Imagistes (who couldn't decide whether they were
English or French) and as far as I am concerned couldn't
write good poetry in either language! Generally
speaking these poets went about trying to give drivel a
respectable front.

One group of poets was called the Vorticists. (I know
it sounds made up for a joke but you can't write that
sort of stuff, it has to be real). Modern Verse has
different names stuck to it now but still dominates
poetic writing and no poet worth spit is considered any
good if you can tell what the poem is about.

I have included the only known Vorticist Beer Poem.
Don't expect to understand all of it but you might get
some of it. And thank your lucky stars there isn't more
where it came from.

Worlds Elide

Death
      Destruction
            Need.
What of the fire?

Pardon?

Shut up, this is a Vorticist poem.

Sorry. Carry on.

Ah.
     You are sorry
          I might be killed

                   by a lorry...

Damn!

What's the matter?

A bloody rhyme got in.

Is that bad?

It's bloody death, mate, to a Vorticist.
The whole point is to avoid anything that is
at all like poetry.

Well, if you say so.
Why not have a pint?

No.
     I cannot lower myself
                 to drink.

The curdled hoards of Marmion await.

I cannot....

Excuse me. Is that a 'no', because I'm going to have another.

Well,
     just a half.
               Just for the laugh.

Damn, a bloody rhyme again.

*Look. Why don't we just have a drink and leave this
Vorticism for a bit. Why not have a pint?*

Well, just one.

Is this short life,

all bereft...

Here you are.

Thanks

...lost on agony's cleft,

Oh, ruddy hell...

Do you have a water feature in your garden?

Yes, actually, we do. We put it in six months ago
after we saw a makeover programme on the telly...

Gervaise St. John Moloney-Sponge

The modern poet abroad.

An example of what they write when they think nobody's looking.

I'll settle for sitting in Nice, forgotten.
I'll settle for success
however ill-begotten.
I'll settle for staying in print
though now thought of by critics as rotten.
I'll settle for being the past
as long as the royalties last.
I'll settle for another sunny drink,
I'll not write anymore, just think.
I'll settle for what I can get -
and yet, and yet...
I hear the beer calling me back.
No, don't be silly, don't fret.
Just settle for what you can get.
Settle for sitting in Nice.

Anonymous (for income tax purposes)

Writing modern verse can actually be profitable. I quote here in full the brilliant and financially successful

'Ode to Television'

a commissioned work. Can you guess who commissioned it?

BE!

BE!!

SEE!!!

Dame Sydney Atterthwaite

BAD POETRY

You may be wondering why you have got so far into such a definitive work as this and not come across LIMERICKS. Well the answer is simple – Limericks aren't poetry and if they were they would be **BAD POETRY!**

The reason Limericks are bad poetry (or not poetry) is because they are formulaic to the point of mental catatonia – can you see Shelley knocking out Limericks, or Keats, or Big Nelly Applegate (the one on the ladies toilet in Bradford bus station doesn't count as Nelly can't remember writing it)? Of course not. And even if they weren't irremediably formulaic they are utterly tarnished by their long association with the vulgar or even the downright obscene. Who the drinker who has not shuddered with shame as some wine drinking lout has suddenly filled the bar with 'There was a young lady from…'? Of course. And, if all that were not enough, Limericks are not poetry (or bad poetry) for one insuperable objection to them being so (or so) – I can never think of a last line that fits!

However, for the low and vulgar element who may have got the Hamburg Free Press edition of this book (written in French of course) here are some that I nearly wrote earlier. You can work on them in your own time.

A beer-loving vicar named Eric
Whose parish was south of North Berwick,
Gazed out at the pews
And announced the good news

———————————— ∼ ————————————

A brewer of beer, name of Bill,
Caught a fever and became very ill.
His factory foreman,
A man name of Norman

———————————— ∼ ————————————

There was a young woman named Nelly
Who thought she was better than Shelley.
"My poems all rhyme,
well, most of the time."

A young man in a flappy serape
Stood at the bar looking happy.
"You may all of you think
That I'm far gone in drink

All flesh is as grass, we are told,
But you don't worry until you grow old.
Once past fifty you think,
There'll be solace in drink

———————————— ∼ ————————————

A barmaid of note, name of Brenda,
Threw out all she thought might offend her.
At the mildest remark
She would often embark

———————————— ∼ ————————————

Oh! Beer drinkers all, please remember
That good will should prevail in December.
So think thoughts good and fine
Of those who drink wine

———————————— ∼ ————————————

A Limerick writer named Lear
Tried to do it without decent beer.
His output substantial
Gave him comfort financial

———————————— ∼ ————————————

THE BEGINNING OF THE END

and a final word from the authors:

Goodbye

Farewell,
we part.
We never liked you
from the start.
Farewell,
we have some little time
together shared.
As if we cared.
Farewell,
go and have a beer
and give a quiet cheer
for publicans and brewers who
keep and make
good beer,
even for the likes of -
you!

Anon and his mate.

That's about it. It's all turned out so differently from the simple:

Yearning

Oh, Dear, I fear,
I require, **BEER!**

Tom

Still, that's literature for you.

And so we come to the end of the beginning of the end - but remember:

Don't bloody well drink and drive.
It isn't funny,
It isn't clever.
Don't drink and drive,
Let everyone survive.

Don't drink and drive
NOT EVER!

Beer drinkers, everywhere.

PART 2 OF THE END

But soft, what glass at yonder table breaks?

It is a serious thinker who reads books all the way to the very end.   His surprise is such that his glass has fallen from his nerveless fingers.   What, is he still dry eyed and reading? It must have been empty!

He starts, he moves, he seems to feel the thrill of life along his keel (or he may have his comb in his back trouser pocket).   He sees into the future - so can you.

Read on....

After the outstanding success of

All the World's a Pub!

(over 10 copies sold, 57 spoiled by spilled beer in the warehouse, 84 stolen and 2 returned with rude remarks in pencil written in the margins) we are following up with the brilliantly titled:

All the World's a Pub! Vol. 2

The publishers are happy to accept submissions of suitable poems but they must be accompanied by the form at the end of this book.

This is your chance to stand alongside Alice Tadcastle, Lenny Spavin, Slattey Lengrow and other greats who have had their work rejected out of hand.

Grab a pen, buy a pint and go to it.

> I submit the following poem in all humility ensuring you that it is original and previously unpublished and written by me in whom the sole copyright resides.

I realise it is not in the same class as the writing in:

All the World's a Pub!

but I offer it in hope for inclusion in:

All the World's a Pub! Vol.2

if such a book is ever published. *You can lie about the second bit but the bit in the box really needs to be TRUE.* Writers of poems chosen for publication will receive a free copy and four cans or bottles of FREE BEER.

Name..

Address...

....

.... post code...........................

send to:

James Green Publishing
2 Newburn Holdings, nr. Berwick upon Tweed,
Northumberland TD15 2LW

Send s.a.e. for acknowledgement of receipt

THE END
OF THE END

Honestly!

82

Using a writing tool that will not slur make your first attempt at a beer poem on this blank page.
(if you think you can see something on this page, a rat or an elephant –
please go home immediately!)

Further futile attempts may be made on the following pages.

Please do not attempt to read your efforts to other drinkers as the management will throw you out if you do.